CW01512509

Original title:
Sallow Wanes Across the Faerie Husk

Author: Daisy Dewi
ISBN HARDBACK: 978-1-80563-443-0
ISBN PAPERBACK: 978-1-80564-964-9

Whims of the Moonlit Whispering Wood

In the heart where shadows play,
The whispering night holds sway,
Each leaf a tale upon the breeze,
The stars dance gently through the trees.

Soft glimmers on the river's skin,
Where secrets of the forest spin,
A silver glow, a hidden path,
Invites the brave to chase the laugh.

Hush now, for the owls are wise,
Their watchful gaze beneath the skies,
In the stillness, magic brews,
Beneath the gaze of ethereal hues.

A sparkling brook hums lullabies,
To weary travelers it complies,
And every step on mossy ground,
Unveils the wonders yet unbound.

When twilight fades and night is old,
The woods unfold their tales untold,
With every shadow, dreams take flight,
In the moonlit whispers of the night.

Echoing Whispers in a Shrouded Grove

In shadows deep where secrets gleam,
The willow bends with whispered dream.
A path unseen, where tales unfold,
Of ghostly forms and hearts so bold.

Through twilight haze, the echoes play,
In every leaf, the past holds sway.
With murmurs soft like silver threads,
They weave the fates of those long dead.

The Faded Brush of Celestial Paint

Upon the canvas, stars drift low,
With colors bright, in silent glow.
Each stroke a wish from ages past,
A fleeting glimpse that fades too fast.

The moon's soft light, a guiding hand,
Caresses dreams, like grains of sand.
Yet time, that thief, will steal away,
The vibrant hues of night to day.

Veils of Mist at the Twilight Edge

As daylight bows to evening's kiss,
The mist enfolds in tranquil bliss.
It dances on the edge of night,
A shimmering cloak, both soft and bright.

Each breath a sigh, a whispered plea,
For all the dreams that long to be.
Through shadows thin, the souls unite,
In twilight's hold, a pure delight.

Captured Echoes of Enchanted Laughter

In glades where laughter used to ring,
The echoes now are whispering.
Each chuckle trapped in time's embrace,
Paints joy within this sacred space.

Beneath the boughs of ancient trees,
The memories sway upon the breeze.
Though voices fade, their warmth remains,
In every heart, the magic reigns.

Fading Echoes of Celestial Dreams

In twilight's hush, where shadows creep,
A whispering sigh, the stars asleep.
Memories dance on the edge of night,
Fading softly, a soft starlight.

Through yon expanse, a comet glides,
Carrying dreams on silken tides.
Echoes of wishes, both near and far,
Caught in the cradle of a falling star.

Hopes alight on the breath of dawn,
In the stillness, all worries are drawn.
Celestial realms, so vast and wide,
Hold the heart's secrets, where dreams abide.

Yet, as morning breaks, they wane from view,
Glimmers of gold in a sky so blue.
Fleeting whispers of a world once known,
In fading echoes, the heart has grown.

So bid adieu to the dreams we keep,
For in waking hours, no longer sleep.
The night retreats to the distant vast,
As echoes linger, then fade at last.

The Graying Light Beneath the Moonlit Canopy

Beneath the glow of a silvered sphere,
The world unfolds, both wondrous and drear.
Trees sway gently in the evening breeze,
Whispering secrets among the leaves.

A blanket of stars, like diamonds spread,
Casts shadows long, where lost dreams tread.
The moonlight dances on the forest floor,
An echoing chorus, forevermore.

Soft sighs of night weave stories old,
Of heroes brave and hearts so bold.
Yet the light fades, begins to dim,
Leaving the night in shadows grim.

Time drips slowly, like dew on grass,
As memories linger, yet seem to pass.
The canopy sways, a haunting sight,
In the graying light of the waning night.

So here we pause, where magic flows,
In every silence, where mystery grows.
Beneath the moon, our souls take flight,
In the graying glow, we find our light.

Dusk's Caress on Fairy Wings

As dusk descends with a gentle sigh,
Fairy wings flutter through the twilight sky.
They weave a tapestry of starlit dreams,
In the soft glow, where moonlight beams.

Whispers of magic, the evening brings,
Nature sings softly, and the heart clings.
To the melodies borne on the night air,
In each note, a promise, a wish laid bare.

Dancers of twilight, in laughter glide,
With every flicker, they drift and slide.
Beneath the ancient oaks, they play,
Chasing shadows that silently sway.

The world slows down, wrapped in embrace,
As dreams take flight in this sacred space.
Dusk holds the magic, a fleeting gift,
On fairy wings, our spirits lift.

So let us linger as the stars ignite,
In the arms of evening, we find delight.
For in dusk's caress, we are reborn,
With whispers of joy in the coming morn.

The Crumbling Realm of Ethereal Visions

In the realm where shadows weave their tales,
Ethereal visions on dusky trails.
Time's brittle fingers touch the ground,
Whispering secrets that must be found.

Once vibrant dreams, now fading light,
Cast in the canvas of endless night.
Figures of hope, they shimmer and sway,
In realms forgotten, they dance and play.

Crumbling stone and ivy's embrace,
Hold remnants of beauty in this lost space.
Echoing laughter, a haunting refrain,
Memories linger like whispers of rain.

Through the mist, we seek the lost stars,
Tracing old paths lined with echoes and scars.
In this fragile world, we wander and roam,
Finding in darkness, a sense of home.

But as dawn beckons with tendrils of gold,
The veil lifts gently, the stories unfold.
In the crumbling realm, our spirits remain,
Bound to the visions that dance in our veins.

Whispers of the Glooming Gossamer

In the twilight where shadows weave,
A tapestry of dreams we believe.
Silent murmurs on the air,
Gossamer whispers of a secret lair.

Beneath the moon's gentle gaze,
Ancient secrets linger in a daze.
The night sings of long-lost tales,
Softly carried on ghostly gales.

Mossy shrouds and crumbled stone,
Guard the treasures left alone.
In every sigh, a story waits,
To unfold across time's gates.

Glimmering threads in the dark,
Dancing softly like a spark.
Each flicker, a wish from the past,
Bound in silence, forever to last.

So listen close, for you might find,
The whispering voices of humankind.
In the glooming depths, secrets reside,
Where the gossamer spirits softly bide.

Shadows Dance on the Luminous Fern

Beneath the canopy, shadows play,
As silver rays of moonlight sway.
The ferns glisten with a radiant sheen,
In the magic of the night, serene.

Whispers weave through emerald leaves,
Tales of joy and heart that grieves.
The dance of shadows, a graceful art,
Painting stories that never part.

Sunbeams vanish, a soft retreat,
Yet in the dark, the world feels sweet.
Echoes of laughter fill the air,
While shadows twirl without a care.

Mossy beds and twilight's glow,
Gently cradle the secrets we know.
In the silent pause, we find the tune,
Of shadows dancing beneath the moon.

The ferns sway in the cool night breeze,
A symphony sung by ancient trees.
In every flicker, nature's delight,
Where shadows forever kiss the light.

The Withering Lament of Shimmering Elders

In the forest deep, wise trees reside,
Their branches arch like stories wide.
Yet in their trunks, a sorrow weaves,
A lament born from rustling leaves.

The shimmering bark, once full of dreams,
Now whispers softly of fading gleams.
Each knot and twist, a memory bound,
Of seasons lost beneath the ground.

Lost in the echoes of the past,
A dance of shadows, fading fast.
The elders sigh in twilight's embrace,
Their whispers linger in time's grace.

Yet hope remains in each tender shoot,
Resilience found in every root.
New stories rise from the somber sleep,
In the heart of the forest, secrets keep.

Shimmering elders, stand so tall,
Holding wisdom in each gnarled thrall.
In their lament, a promise we see,
Life's cycle shall always find a key.

Twilight's Breath in the Enchanted Grove

In the grove where shadows nap,
Twilight weaves a soft, warm wrap.
A breath of magic lingers near,
In every rustle, a tale to hear.

The leaves shimmer with droplet hues,
Carried forth by the evening muse.
Beneath the sky, a dance unfolds,
In whispers soft, the night beholds.

The stars awaken, blink with grace,
Lighting the path in a boundless space.
As shadows mingle, secrets blend,
In twilight's breath, the dreams ascend.

Glimmers of hope in the dusk's caress,
The grove sings sweet, a soft success.
Each moment blooms, a fleeting rhyme,
Captured softly in the hands of time.

So linger here where spirits dwell,
In the enchanted grove, all is well.
For twilight breathes a gentle sigh,
Wrapping the night in a dreamer's eye.

The Echo of a Fading So.

the Glen

In twilight's grasp, a whisper
A melody of dreams long ɪ,
Through ancient trees, it gently s
In harmony with fading days.

Each note a tale of time long gone,
Of laughter lost, of love's sweet song.
The glen remembers every tune,
Beneath the gaze of a crescent moon.

Yet shadows dance where footsteps stray,
In echoes soft, they fade away.
A memory lingers, bright yet pale,
A song that weaves a wistful tale.

With every breeze, a sigh will rise,
As stars awaken in velvet skies.
The glen embraces each refrain,
A wistful waltz amidst the rain.

Legends Underneath the Canopy
Glimmer

In the boughs where secrets dwell,
Whispers of heroes weave their spell.
In shadows deep, the stories gleam,
A tapestry of forgotten dreams.

The rustling leaves, a silent pact,
With every breeze, they softly act.
Guardians of lore, they gently sway,
In twilight's shade, they softly play.

Glimmers twine in the dappled light,
Awakening legends of ancient might.
With every rustle, a voice anew,
In the heart of the forest, they call to you.

Once bravest knights, now spirits roam,
In search of those who call them home.
The canopy holds their tales so dear,
In whispers hushed, we long to hear.

Shadows of Enchantment Beneath a Dying Sky

Beneath the hues of dusk's embrace,
Shadows dance in a whispered grace.
The twilight hums a secret tune,
In colors fading like a moon.

As stars appear in the velvet shroud,
A nightingale sings, soft yet loud.
Enchantments swirl in the evening air,
As magic lingers with quiet care.

The world holds its breath, a silent plea,
For moments caught in tranquility.
Yet in the dark, where wonders lie,
Shadows weave beneath the dying sky.

Each flicker of light, a fleeting spark,
Revealing dreams in the vast dark.
Beneath the stars, we seek and find,
The magic lost to a wandering mind.

The Riddle of the Shimmering Night

When evening falls with a gentle sigh,
The night unfurls its blanket high.
In silver threads, the stars are spun,
A riddle waits for hearts to run.

The moonbeams whisper, secrets tight,
Enticing souls to take flight.
With every gleam, a question sways,
In the riddle of the shimmering haze.

Dreamers roam with lanterns bright,
Chasing shadows in the velvet night.
Each flicker bears a tale untold,
In mystery's grasp, we dare be bold.

A whisper soft, a lingering glance,
Inviting hearts to join the dance.
In the riddles spun by the silver light,
We find our truth in the shimmering night.

Whispers of Dusk's Embrace

As daylight wanes, the shadows play,
Whispers of dusk steal light away.
Crickets sing in a soft refrain,
Stars awaken, bright and plain.

The moon hangs low, a silvery friend,
Wrapping the world in dreams to bend.
A breeze carries secrets, gentle and light,
In the stillness of approaching night.

Through rustling leaves, old tales unfurl,
Of magic hidden in the twilight swirl.
Each moment brews a tale long spun,
In the quiet realm where dreams have run.

Dusk paints the skies in hues of grace,
Softly cradling the world's embrace.
In the heart of dusk, we find our way,
As whispers linger till break of day.

With every breath, we feel the shift,
A lingering spell, a wondrous gift.
In this twilight, we gather our fears,
And let them dance through the night's tears.

Shadows on the Gossamer Path

Upon the gossamer path we tread,
In shadows deep, where secrets are bred.
Moonlight weaves through branches bare,
Guiding us gently, unaware.

Footfalls muted as magic stirs,
In the air, enchantment purrs.
Every corner holds a sigh,
Stories waiting, long since dry.

A flicker of light, a whispered name,
In the dance of shadows, nothing's the same.
The night unveils tales of yore,
Lurking gently behind the door.

Beneath the stars, our hearts take flight,
Chasing dreams in the soft twilight.
Every step brings tales anew,
On this path where shadows grew.

And though the night may hide in veil,
Hope blooms bright with dreams to sail.
We walk together, hand in hand,
On the gossamer path, in twilight's land.

Twilight's Breath in the Enchanted Vale

In the vale where twilight streams,
The air is thick with ancient dreams.
Veils of fog caress the trees,
Whispering softly on the breeze.

A symphony of crickets calls,
Echoing through the castle walls.
Each note trails like a silver thread,
Binding together what's long since said.

Ferns unfurl with a sleepy yawn,
In twilight's breath, a new day's dawn.
With every glance, enchantments twine,
In the mysterious glow, we align.

Fireflies dance in a starlit waltz,
A glimpse of magic, a hidden pulse.
Each flicker hints of worlds unspoken,
In the vale where hearts are woken.

And as the sun dips low, unseen,
The vale awakens, lush and green.
In twilight's arms, we come alive,
Where every moment helps us thrive.

Luminous Echoes of Forgotten Dreams

In the twilight hour, dreams align,
Luminous echoes through the pine.
Whispers of wishes left behind,
In the night sky, stars entwined.

The past flutters like a breath of air,
Carrying hopes beyond despair.
In the embrace of night's soft glow,
Forgotten dreams begin to flow.

With every flicker, the heart will soar,
Journeying back to what came before.
In the silence, shadows take flight,
Painting memories in soft moonlight.

Each heartbeat sings a tender song,
Stitching the night where we belong.
The echoes of laughter swirl around,
In the dreamscape, solace is found.

As dawn approaches, the dreams may fade,
Yet in our hearts, the light is laid.
Carry the whispers, hold them tight,
Luminous echoes guide us through night.

The Lure of Diminished Glow

In twilight's grasp, the shadows creep,
Where whispers dance and secrets seep.
The lanterns flicker, dimmed by time,
A haunting song, a distant chime.

Beneath the boughs, the memories sway,
Of laughter lost, of games we play.
With every breath, the night unfolds,
A tapestry of stories told.

The stars above, like eyes, they gleam,
In corners dark, where wishful dreams.
Yet still we chase the fleeting light,
To banish cold and greet the night.

Oh, wander forth, ye hearts so bold,
Embrace the warmth against the cold.
For in the mist, the magic stirs,
With every choice, the heartbeat whirs.

In shadows deep, find strength anew,
A whisper here, a promise true.
The lure of glow, though dimmed it seems,
Awakens gently all our dreams.

Brooding Silence Across the Faerie Glens

In glens where faeries tiptoe light,
The silence weaves through day and night.
With every breeze, a tale unfolds,
Of ancient paths and mysteries bold.

The brooding trees, their branches twist,
In shadows deep, where sunbeams missed.
They guard the whispers on the wind,
Of secrets lost and hearts rescind.

Embroidered glades of emerald hue,
Hide realms where magic once rang true.
Yet all is still, the echoes faint,
In the soft sigh of nature's plaint.

Upon the stones, the dew does weep,
For dreams that linger in their sleep.
A call to those who dare to seek,
In every nook, in every peak.

Ethereal glimmers catch the eye,
Yet silence reigns beneath the sky.
The faerie glens, so brooding, bare,
Invite the brave to breathe their air.

Threads of Fate Woven with Darkness

In twilight's weave, the fates entwine,
Each thread of darkness, every line.
A tapestry of choice unfolds,
With whispers low, with stories bold.

Among the looms, the shadows play,
As destiny holds sway today.
The tapestry sings a solemn song,
Of right and wrong, of where we belong.

The weaver's hand, both deft and sure,
Creates a map, both dark and pure.
With every stitch, a journey wrought,
In silence kept, in battles fought.

The threads may fray, the colors bleed,
Yet still we tread, intent to heed.
For life is sewn with fortitude,
A dance of light and solitude.

So hold the strands, both bright and black,
With every breath, do not look back.
For in the shadows, hope will gleam,
And weave into our sweetest dream.

Eclipsed Dreams in the Mossy Hollow

In mossy hollow, dreams take flight,
Yet shadows cast a fleeting blight.
Eclipsed by doubts that linger near,
The heart's true wish begins to sear.

Amid the ferns, a whisper calls,
In muted tones, where silence falls.
The beckoning mist, the silver light,
Draws forth the dreams concealed from sight.

Beneath the arch of ancient trees,
Find solace in the gentle breeze.
With every breath, let hopes revive,
In whispered vows, our souls contrive.

The hollow holds both light and gloom,
A sanctuary carved from doom.
Yet in its depths, a spark ignites,
To chase the dark and summon nights.

Eclipsed, unfurl each hidden thought,
In moonlit glades, where truths are sought.
For in this realm, with courage strewn,
The dreams will rise beneath the moon.

The Dimmed Glow of Lost Lullabies

The moon whispered softly, a lullaby weak,
In shadows it flickered, the night seemed to speak.
Stars blinked like tears on a velvet expanse,
While dreams drifted gently, in forgotten dance.

Once vibrant and warm, now a dimmed glow,
Echoes of laughter, like whispers of snow.
The cradle of night cradles time's tender song,
Yet memories linger, where they once did belong.

Windows are darkened, the curtains drawn tight,
Where echoes of childhood fade into night.
With each passing moment, the whispers grow faint,
As illusions retreat in the silence we paint.

Caught in the silence, a heart learns to grieve,
For lullabies lost, and the dreams we believe.
Yet deep in the stillness, a spirit may rise,
Finding the glow in the dawn of new skies.

So cherish each moment, let not the light fade,
For lullabies hold all the hopes we have laid.
In the dim glow of night, let the heart gently sigh,
For dreams are just stardust, awaiting to fly.

Shattered Dreams on the Edge of Enchantment

Beneath the bright moon, where shadows conspire,
Lay dreams woven soft, wrapped in twilight's choir.
But whispers of doubt twist the fabric once spun,
As laughter once joyous drifts into the run.

A dance of illusions atop fragile glass,
Each step feels like thunder, as bright visions pass.
With echoes of magic, now splintered and torn,
Once vibrant imaginations, now weathered and worn.

On the edge of the twilight, where longing takes hold,
Fate's threads weave a tapestry, tattered and bold.
Hopes flutter like moths, drawn to flames of despair,
Yet deep in the darkness, there's strength in the air.

Chasing the shadows, we wander alone,
Searching for fragments of what once was home.
Though dreams may be shattered, and pathways unclear,
Magic still lingers, beckoning near.

As dawn breaks upon us, casting light on our fears,
We gather the pieces, through laughter and tears.
On the edge of enchantment, let courage redeem,
For even in darkness, we chase down our dream.

Flickering Shadows in the Faerie Thicket

In the heart of the thicket, where secrets reside,
Flickering shadows, where the faeries hide.
Each glimmer of light dances softly through trees,
Whispers of magic upon the cool breeze.

Glimpses of laughter and flickers of grace,
In a world wrapped in wonder, we find our own place.
Yet shadows may linger, pulling dreams to the dark,
Chasing away echoes of the heart's gentle spark.

Paths twist and turn, like the stories we weave,
Lost in the thicket, believing, we leave.
For every dark shadow hides a flicker of light,
An ember of hope that shines boldly at night.

Amidst the enchantment, where wishes may wane,
The faeries are waiting, amidst joy and pain.
With courage ignited, we step through the veil,
To find the true magic that lies in the tale.

So dance through the shadows, embrace every twist,
For even in darkness, there's magic to list.
In the flickering moments, let the heart ignite,
For shadows bring depth to the shimmering light.

The Pale Remnants of a Fading Tale

Once spun with bright colors, now fading to gray,
Lies the tale of our youth, drifting further away.
Where whispers of laughter once filled the soft air,
Now silence invades, a lamenting affair.

Each page worn and tattered, like dreams left behind,
Remnants of stories, once bold and aligned.
Yet even in twilight, new tales may arise,
From ashes of shadows, to brightening skies.

With ghosts of the past, where memory strays,
We gather the pieces, in luminous rays.
In the hushed quiet moments, a new story waits,
Awakening softly, as the heart resonates.

For every great ending summons a new start,
Even faded will tales can revive a lost heart.
Thus from pale remnants, like bloom from the tree,
A tapestry woven in the lives yet to be.

So let not the shadows obscure what we find,
In fading tales, treasures of heart intertwined.
For stories still linger like echoes in halls,
A testament born from the magic in all.

The Weaving of Faded Tapestries

In threads of gold and silver spun,
Ancient tales of battles won.
Whispers linger, shadows play,
In faded fabrics held at bay.

With needles kissed by twilight's grace,
Each stitch recalls a fleeting face.
The loom's soft hum sings of yore,
Of dreams long lost on distant shore.

Time dances lightly, soft and wise,
In each pattern, secrets rise.
Beneath the warp where magic flows,
Life's tapestry ever grows.

Yet dust may settle on the seams,
Dimming once-bright daydream streams.
But in the heart, the colors blend,
Reviving tales that never end.

So let us weave till night is done,
In the quiet where magic's spun.
For in the threads both old and new,
The weaver is me, and the weaver is you.

Phantoms of Whimsy Under a Clouded Sky

Beneath the gray, a shimmer hides,
Where playful spirits slip, like tides.
They dance and laugh in veils of mist,
A fleeting joy too sweet to list.

With moonbeams weaving through the dark,
Bright laughter echoes, swift and stark.
In the corners of our dreams,
The phantoms tease with whispered schemes.

They paint the clouds in colors wild,
A riddle's game, a dreamer's child.
Within the hush, they leave a trace,
A stitch of wonder, a glimpse of grace.

In twilight's breath, they intertwine,
With wishes spun on silver line.
Each sigh a spark, each glance a cue,
To seek the magic, born anew.

So let us chase those fabled sprites,
Through shadowed paths and starry nights.
For in their flight, our spirits rise,
To dance with phantoms 'neath clouded skies.

Secrets Told by the Evening Mist

When twilight drapes her velvet cloak,
Whispers stir the silence, soft and woke.
The evening mist, a shroud of lore,
Hides ancient truths once told before.

With every breath, the secrets creep,
Into the hearts that dare to leap.
Ghost stories swirl on gentle breeze,
Unraveling time with each tease.

The world grows still, as shadows blend,
In twilight's realm where dreams transcend.
From moonlit glades to starlit streams,
The mist reveals our hidden dreams.

Each dewdrop glistens, a world inside,
A glimpse of hope where dreams abide.
In layers deep, the past unfolds,
Mysteries wrapped in stories told.

So let us wander through this night,
And listen close to the soft delight.
For in the mist, the heart can find,
The secrets held by the night entwined.

Embracing the Void Between Worlds

In whispered dusk, where shadows part,
We find the edge of the unknown heart.
Between the realms, a space to glide,
To dance upon the shifting tide.

Where silence hums, and echoes freeze,
In the void, we drift with ease.
A bridge of thought, a realm untold,
In twilight's grasp, we will be bold.

Beyond the stars, where dreams collide,
In teardrops lost, and laughter wide.
We gather light from every sigh,
Where moments flourish, time flies high.

With every heartbeat, worlds embrace,
A tender weave in a timeless space.
For in this void, both strange and bright,
We find our truth, our guiding light.

So let us sail through dark and bright,
To cherish all that stirs the night.
For in the gaps, the magic swirls,
In the tender void, between our worlds.

A Whisper from the Fern-Covered Hollow

In the hush of the emerald glade,
Whispers of magic twine and fade.
Softly the ferns embrace the night,
As shadows dance in silver light.

Secrets murmur through the trees,
Carried gently on the breeze.
Each leaf holds tales of yore,
Of enchantments, of ancient lore.

Beneath the boughs where dreams align,
Hope ignites like a beacon divine.
With each step on the mossy floor,
Hearts entwined, we seek for more.

A flicker sparks in the cool, dark air,
A haunting tune, a whispered prayer.
In ferns of green, we find our way,
To the heart of night, where wishes sway.

So linger here, if but a while,
Let the forest claim your smile.
For in this hollow, far from strife,
Awaits the magic of pure life.

Hues of Memory on the Sylvan Path

Upon the path where shadows play,
Colors of twilight softly sway.
Cascading leaves in golden hues,
Paint the world in ancient views.

Each step recalls a whispered dream,
Fragments woven like a seam.
Sunlight dapples on the ground,
In the hearts of trees, tales abound.

With every rustle, time stands still,
Echoes linger, a vibrant thrill.
Petals fall like forgotten lore,
Reminders of what came before.

As twilight deepens, shadows blend,
The sylvan path will never end.
In hues of memory, we tread light,
Guided by starlit, shimmering night.

Let the whispers in the breeze,
Fill your soul with gentle ease.
For on this way, each heart shall find,
A treasure trove of the intertwined.

Enigmas in the Flickering Glow of Starlight

In the stillness of the azure night,
Stars unveil secrets, shining bright.
Mysteries dance with the faintest gleam,
Weaving around us a silvery dream.

What tales do the heavens choose to share?
Whispers echo in the cool night air.
Every flicker, a pulse of fate,
A yearning heart, it cannot wait.

Cloaked in shadows, yet aglow,
Stars hold the truths we long to know.
Time slows down; the world feels wide,
As we are drawn to the cosmic tide.

Among the constellations' weave,
We trace the paths of those who believe.
In the flickering light, we find our way,
An enigma that haunts the night and day.

With each twinkle, a wish shall soar,
To realms unknown, and evermore.
In starlight's grasp, we dare to dream,
Beyond the darkness, through the seam.

Chase of the Dying Horizon

In the twilight's final embrace,
We chase the sun, a fleeting grace.
Colors bleed; the sky ignites,
Echoes of day in dazzling flights.

With every step, we reach for gold,
Chasing stories yet untold.
The horizon whispers soft and low,
Promises wrapped in twilight glow.

Clouds drift by like whispered dreams,
Carried on the wind's gentle streams.
As day unravels, shadows grow,
The chase continues, an endless flow.

Night unfolds, a velvet cloak,
As stars awaken, words unspoke.
A final glance, goodbye to light,
Into the arms of encroaching night.

But in this chase, we find the spark,
In every moment, tracing the arc.
For though the sun may dip and wane,
In heart, its warmth shall still remain.

The Last Gleam of Once-Blooming Fables

In gardens where shadows softly lay,
The fables once whispered have faded away.
Remember the laughter that danced in the air,
Now echoes of silence drift low everywhere.

A blossom once vibrant, now crumples to dust,
Each story, a whisper, entangled in rust.
The pages of ages, yellowed and torn,
Hold secrets of dreams that the world has not worn.

The starlight still twinkles, a flicker of hope,
In memories wrapped like a delicate rope.
The heart gently weaves through the tangle of time,
Seeking the music of forgotten rhyme.

Yet in dying embers, a spark can ignite,
To light the lost paths that lead to the night.
For even in endings, new tales may begin,
In the last gleam of fables, a new story spins.

Threads of Twilight in the Enchanted Thicket

In the thicket where twilight weaves gentle spells,
Whispers of magic in soft, hidden wells.
The branches embrace the fading daylight,
While secrets of shadows awaken at night.

The murmurs of petals unfold like a sigh,
As dreams dance on edges of whispering sky.
Each twinkle of starlight, a thread in the seam,
Winding through pathways of silvery dream.

With every lost echo, the forest will hum,
A melody timeless, like distant drums.
The heart beats in rhythm with nature's own song,
In the thicket where all of the wonders belong.

Beneath the soft canopy, stories take flight,
In twilight's embrace, the new world ignites.
With threads spun of wonder, await the dawn's glow,
In the hush of enchanted twilight, we grow.

The Fable Woven by Whispering Winds

The winds carry tales on their wisping breath,
Of heroes and lovers, of life and of death.
They swirl in the night, a soft, haunting sound,
Woven in silence, where lost dreams are bound.

Through valleys and hills, the breezes will roam,
Each whisper a promise, each sigh a home.
The ear can hear secrets, if still it will be,
For fables are spoken in notes of the free.

Touched by the twilight, embraced by the dawn,
In the fabric of air, where silence has drawn.
The voices interlace in a dance so divine,
A tapestry woven through space and through time.

Let not the heart stray from the song of the wind,
For life's sweetest tales often too will rescind.
Yet every soft breath, every fleeting sigh,
Is a fable retold as the moments drift by.

Silhouettes of Dreams in the Wisping Mist

In a world draped in mystery, the mist gently sways,
Shrouding the shadows in silvery grays.
Silhouettes of dreams come alive in the haze,
Where time loops and dances in delicate ways.

Each figure a story, each ghost a soft sigh,
Echoes of longings that dare to fly high.
The heart swells with wonder as dusk settles deep,
In the arms of the night where the lost moments weep.

With a flutter of hope, the dreams softly tread,
In landscapes of twilight where wishes are led.
The mist cloaks the worlds that were born from our fears,
Transforming the shadows to light through our tears.

So dance with the phantoms, let whispers embrace,
In the stillness of night, find your own hidden place.
For in silhouettes woven with strands of the mist,
Lie stories forgotten, waiting to be kissed.

The Lullaby of Dwindling Light

As shadows stretch and whisper low,
The gentle winds begin to blow.
Stars awaken, shyly bright,
In the cradle of the night.

The moon's soft glow, a silver thread,
Weaves through dreams that softly spread.
In the quiet, secrets soar,
Dancing lightly to the shore.

Close your eyes, let worries fade,
In the twilight's warm parade.
Hushed are hearts beneath the sky,
Where long-lost wishes softly lie.

Embrace the calm, the dusk's sweet song,
In this place, you still belong.
Nature's sighs, a tender balm,
Wrap you in the evening's calm.

So drift away, let starlight guide,
Through realms where dreams and hopes abide.
With each breath, let love ignite,
In the lullaby of dwindling light.

Fleeting Moments in the Enchanted Twilight

In twilight's glow, all things unite,
Mysterious hues adorn the night.
Fleeting whispers touch the trees,
Carried forth on gentle breeze.

The fireflies dance with tender grace,
Illuminating nature's face.
Moments blend, both sweet and rare,
As time suspends its silent stare.

Within this hour, secrets dwell,
Stories weave their timeless spell.
Every glance, a world anew,
Fleeting moments, pure and true.

The stars align, a cosmic sigh,
Echoes linger in the sky.
Every heartbeat, a melody,
In this realm of fantasy.

As twilight deepens, dreams take flight,
Painting wonders in the night.
Hold these moments, let them stay,
In the magic of the day.

Echoes of the Ethereal Grove

Beneath the trees, where shadows weave,
The world transforms, if you believe.
Whispers linger in the air,
Echoing secrets everywhere.

The ethereal grove, a sacred space,
Holds the essence of time and place.
Dancing leaves in harmony,
Singing songs of mystery.

Fables rise from roots so deep,
Guarding dreams while others sleep.
Every rustle tells a tale,
Of magic lost along the trail.

The stars above, a watchful eye,
Guide the wanderers passing by.
In each echo, history flows,
As the heart of nature knows.

So venture forth, let spirits roam,
In the grove that feels like home.
With every step, let wonders grow,
In the echoes of the grove.

The Dusk Before the Phantom Dawn

The dusk arrives, the colors bleed,
With shadows long, our hearts take heed.
A tender veil embraces night,
Before the dawn that hides from sight.

In whispered tones, the world prepares,
For magic spun in twilight airs.
Each moment holds a hidden grace,
A sacred dance, a timeless space.

The horizon glimmers, dreams alight,
Treading softly through the night.
As echoes linger, whispers tread,
In the dreams where hope is bred.

With every heartbeat, time suspends,
As dusk and dawn shall meet as friends.
In this fleeting hour, we breathe,
Every longing, every weave.

So gather close, behold the light,
In the dusk before the phantom night.
For every ending, new begins,
In the dance where magic spins.

Journey Into the Veil of Shadows

In twilight's grasp, we wander wide,
Through whispering woods where secrets bide.
The air is thick with echoes faint,
As lanterns flicker, shadows paint.

Beneath the boughs where phantoms sigh,
Old stories linger, memories lie.
A path of dreams and whispers flows,
Where none but the brave dare to go.

With every step, the night unfolds,
Its grasp of magic, tightly holds.
Muffled cries and laughter blend,
In the realm where realities bend.

The moon casts spells on ancient stone,
Illuminating the love we've known.
And as we tread on hollow ground,
The heart of the shadows beats profound.

Haunting Harmonies of the Moonlit Meadow

In meadows bright where moonbeams play,
The nightingale sings a soft ballet.
Each note a whisper of love's embrace,
Floating gently in this tranquil space.

The daisies nod in silver light,
As shadows dance with delicate might.
A breeze carries tales of long ago,
While stars above put on a show.

With twinkling eyes, the owls observe,
In search of stories yet to serve.
They hoot a lonesome serenade,
As night wraps all in softened shade.

The cool earth breathes in silent sighs,
While fireflies flicker like wishing skies.
In the heart of darkness, beauty gleams,
A haunting harmony that dreams.

The Ethereal Dance Before Nightfall

As daylight wanes, the shadows grow,
A rhythmic dance begins to flow.
With every twirl, the world is spun,
In an ethereal chase, we come undone.

The trees sway gracefully, arms held high,
While clouds drift slow in the dusky sky.
A melody rises, soft and sweet,
Inviting all to the twilight's beat.

Despite the looming edge of dark,
There's magic in this fleeting spark.
Each creature joins in joyous trance,
Lost in the beauty of twilight's dance.

In every heartbeat, nature calls,
The night awaits as daylight falls.
A fleeting glance, a chance to feel,
The night's embrace, a world surreal.

Tales of the Unseen Dusk

In every dusky hue, a tale is spun,
Of shadows whispering when day is done.
The secrets tucked in twilight's fold,
Are stories of wonder waiting to be told.

Beneath the stars that gently gleam,
Lies the unseen path of every dream.
A journey through the veil of night,
Where fantasy and reality ignite.

The breeze carries fragments of forgotten lore,
Echoing softly from long before.
A pulse of magic fills the air,
Entwining the bold with those unaware.

So listen close as the shadows weave,
The fabric of tales that none believe.
In dusk's embrace, where silence speaks,
Unseen truths is what the heart seeks.

Haunting Chimes of the Geraldine Glade

In Geraldine's embrace, the chimes do sway,
Echoing secrets of night and day.
Whispers of shadows, they dance and twirl,
A melody woven in a mystic whirl.

Through emerald leaves, the soft notes play,
Tales of the forest where fairies stray.
Each sound a reminder, a tale retold,
Of ancient magic, of dreams of gold.

The winds carry laughter, the wildflowers nod,
In the glade where footsteps on dew are trod.
The chimes ring clear though the world may fade,
In whispered echoes, the past is laid.

With each haunting bell, a shiver ignites,
Awakening spirits of long-lost nights.
In Geraldine Glade, where shadows entwine,
The chimes sing a chorus, so hauntingly divine.

The Soft Murmurs of Dissolution

In twilight's embrace, when day bids adieu,
Soft murmurs of change drift gently in view.
Nature weaves whispers, secrets unfold,
As shadows dissolve the stories of old.

The river flows softly, a tune low and sweet,
Each ripple a memory, a pulse in retreat.
Moonlight caresses the world's fading sigh,
While stars twinkle softly like dreams passing by.

In the quiet of dusk, the colors do fade,
The night wraps its cloak 'round the glen and glade.
With every breath taken, the stillness grows deep,
As the whispers of twilight cradle the sleep.

These murmurs remind us of journeys begun,
Of laughter and heartache, of battles won.
In the echoes of dusk, we find solace near,
As dissolution brings forth a beauty sincere.

Shadows Beckon in the Mossy Alcove

Beneath ancient trees, where shadows do play,
In mossy alcoves, the spirits stay.
With whispers so soft, they beckon and call,
Inviting the wanderer, inviting us all.

The air thick with magic, both secret and rare,
Entwined with the echoes of stories laid bare.
Moonbeams dapple softly on wet, emerald hue,
As the shadows invite tales older than dew.

Through twigs and through brambles, a path we will find,

Where the heart of the forest speaks to the mind.
Each footstep a promise, each glance a new tale,
As shadows like whispers in twilight unveil.

In this sacred retreat, where silence abounds,
We listen for murmurs, for lost, sacred sounds.
The alcove awaits those who dare to believe,
That shadows can cradle the dreams we conceive.

Disappearing Rays of Forgotten Magic

In the fading light, where the sun bids farewell,
Disappearing rays weave a mystical spell.
With fingers of gold, they caress the leaves,
Yet linger just briefly before the night weaves.

Forgotten magic stirs, deep in the glen,
Where stories of wonder awaken again.
Each flicker of light holds a tale of the past,
A flicker of hope that forever will last.

In twilight's embrace, the whispers ignite,
Like fireflies dancing, igniting the night.
The magic may fade, but the heart will hold tight,
To rays of remembrance, casting shadows so bright.

With every soft shimmer that leaves us so bare,
We cherish the moments like treasures laid there.
In the heart of the dusk, where magic resides,
The disappearing rays weave the dreams that still guide.

Murmurs Lost in the Enchanted Mist

Whispers float on the cool night air,
Flickering lights in shadows' stare.
Dancing thoughts in the twilight's embrace,
Echoed secrets that time can't erase.

Beneath the boughs of ancient trees,
Lies a magic carried on the breeze.
Voices woven with silver threads,
Stirring dreams while the daylight dreads.

Lurking shadows where dreams collide,
In the hush where the memories bide.
Murmurs call from the depths unseen,
Hints of the past where the heart once keen.

In the mist, a soft laughter rings,
Magic lingers, on delicate wings.
With each sigh, the night's song unfurls,
In enchanted realms where wonder twirls.

Forever echoing in the night,
Lost to the world, yet holding tight.
Murmurs drift, a gentle kiss,
Goodbye to the day, and hello to bliss.

Time's Tattered Veil in the Faery Realm

In the realm where the shadows play,
Time weaves secrets that fade away.
Tattered threads of a silken dream,
Whispered tales that are rarely seen.

Luminous glimmers of ages past,
Glide on whispers, shadows cast.
Moments captured in fleeting light,
Held within the faery's flight.

Among the blooms where dreams take root,
The wild faeries dance in their pursuit.
Time spins softly, a delicate lace,
Drawing us in to a timeless space.

Haunting echoes of laughter and joy,
Resonate deep like a loved one's toy.
Where wishes whisper, and hopes entwine,
In time's tattered veil, all is divine.

Yet shadows linger, a hum of fate,
Threads unraveling at destiny's gate.
With every tick of the clock's soft chime,
Echoes of magic evade their prime.

Eclipsed Reflections of Forgotten Souls

In the twilight's grasp, shadows arise,
Eclipsed reflections in moonlit skies.
Haunting the edges of sight and sound,
Forgotten souls dance, unbound.

Flickering glimpses of what once was,
Moments captured in a gentle pause.
Silhouettes whisper of tales untold,
Shimmering faintly, both wary and bold.

Threads of sorrow and laughter blend,
In the realm where the lost transcend.
Beneath starry veils, they weave and twirl,
Forgotten dreams in an endless swirl.

Mirrors crack with a ghostly sigh,
Reflections shimmer then say goodbye.
In the dusk of the heart's hidden fold,
Lies a yearning for stories of old.

These souls intertwine with the cries of the night,
Filling the silence with soft, silver light.
In eclipsed reflections, they softly cling,
To the echoes of joy that the darkness brings.

Moth Eaten Threads of Verdant Sorcery

In the forest deep where shadows twine,
Moth-eaten threads of magic align.
Casting spells in the dappled light,
A tapestry woven from day into night.

Leaves murmur secrets in earthy tones,
Nature's whimsy, a symphony of bones.
Specters of green haunt the wilting brume,
Verdant sorcery weaving the gloom.

From petals soft, cadences breathe,
Whispering tales of the heart's reprieve.
Threads frail and worn tell stories anew,
In every sigh, life's essence rings true.

Beneath the arch of the ancient trees,
Soars a magic carried on the breeze.
Moth-eaten threads trap a glimmering spark,
Crafted by shadows that dance in the dark.

Through teeming life, let enchantments blend,
In the heart of the forest, on wonders depend.
With every breath, the song takes its flight,
In moth-eaten threads, we find our light.

Ghostly Echoes in the Twilight Glade

In shadows where the whispers play,
The trees hold secrets night and day.
A flicker, a sigh, the soft moon's gaze,
Echoes linger in a mystic haze.

Footsteps tread on ancient ground,
Where lost souls in silence abound.
With every rustle, a tale unfolds,
Of wishes whispered, and dreams retold.

Beneath the boughs, the specters dance,
In shimmering light, they take their chance.
Haunting melodies fill the air,
A lullaby spun with shadows rare.

Through gnarled roots and ferny beds,
The glade where time itself is shed.
In ghostly realms where night prevails,
Lives the magic of soft, silent tales.

So heed the call, the beckoning night,
Discover the dreams, bring forth the light.
In twilight's glade, let your heart be free,
For there you'll find your own legacy.

The Vanishing Starlit Path

In the woods where darkness beckons,
A path once bright, now fades and lessens.
Stars dance gently like whispered sighs,
Each step unravels the night's disguise.

Where starlight flickers, shadows blend,
A journey lost, but not the end.
With every breath, the magic swells,
In the heart of night, where silence dwells.

The moon, a guide with silver sheen,
Illuminates sights yet to be seen.
A fleeting dream on the edge of sight,
The path dissolves in twinkling light.

Whispers call from the depths beyond,
Echoes of journeys that feel so fond.
Each step a story, each turn a chance,
To reclaim the wonder in night's romance.

So follow the glow that softly glints,
With faith aglow and heart that hints.
For within the dark, there's beauty's grace,
On the vanishing path, find your place.

Rhythms of the Somber Sylphs

In the hush of night where secrets weave,
Somber sylphs in shadows grieve.
Their whispers play on the cool night air,
A melody woven with ethereal flair.

With phantom wings and gentle sighs,
They twirl through the stars in twilight skies.
Each movement spills a haunting tune,
A symphony sung under the moon.

Lost in a dance of graceful despair,
These spirits sigh with a burdened care.
They cradled dreams that slipped away,
In shimmering dusk of the fading day.

Through forests deep where lost hopes trail,
The sylphs recount their silvered tale.
Eternally bound to the night's embrace,
In sorrow's rhythm, they find their place.

So linger awhile in their mournful song,
Where spirits twine and shadows throng.
The rhythms of sylphs in twilight unfold,
An echo of stories forever retold.

The Decaying Embrace of Lucent Fables

In whispers soft, where legends lie,
The fables flicker and slowly die.
Once bright as dawn, now faded grey,
In shadows' clutch, they waste away.

Twilight weaves through tales long told,
Of heroes brave and treasures bold.
Yet time's cruel hand, with gentle theft,
Steals the glow from the stories left.

In crumbling tomes and dusty lore,
The echoes of laughter haunt the shore.
A glimmering past now worn and frail,
Where vibrant joys begin to pale.

But still they linger, those tales of old,
In memory's heart, their warmth enfold.
For even as dust on pages lay,
The spirit of fables shall never stray.

So cherish the stories that time may wear,
In the decaying embrace, be aware.
For each faded tale, though lost in the past,
Holds the promise that true dreams can last.

Chasing Phantoms Through the Thicket

In the heart of the woods, shadows creep,
Whispers of magic, where secrets sleep.
Haunting the trails where the wild things roam,
Chasing the phantoms that call this place home.

Moonlight flickers through branches' embrace,
Echoes of laughter, a familiar face.
Footsteps that linger, soft as a sigh,
Guiding the lost like the stars in the sky.

A rustle, a glimmer, a shimmer of hope,
Twisting and turning, a soft, fragile rope.
Bound by enchantment, the air heavy still,
Each turn revealing a glimmering thrill.

Winding through pathways where night creatures sing,
Under the gaze of the silver-winged king.
With every heartbeat, the thicket weaves tight,
A tapestry woven from shadows and light.

Embrace the unknown, let your spirit take flight,
In the dance of the phantoms, lost to the night.
For those who dare wander, a journey begins,
Through thicket and twilight, where the brave always win.

Remnants of a Starlit Reverie

When the day fades to whispers of light,
Dreams weave like clouds, soft and bright.
Beneath the vast heavens, secrets unfold,
Remnants of tales in starlight told.

A canvas of wishes, painted in night,
Shimmering whispers giving hearts flight.
Lost in the echoes of time's gentle call,
Holding the memories that flutter and fall.

Each twinkle a memory, sweet and sincere,
Guiding the lost through the shroud of their fear.
The laughter of starlight, a comforting sound,
Cradles the world, deep magic unbound.

As dawn breaks the spell, shadows retreat,
The remnants of reverie taste bittersweet.
But in every sunrise, a promise anew,
The stars will return, shining brightly for you.

So dream the lost dreams, let your heart soar,
For beneath the starlit sky, there's always more.
In the whispers of twilight, our souls start to dance,
In the remnants of dreams, we find our romance.

Ensnared by a Dying Light

In the twilight hour, where shadows blend,
The world slows its breath, hearts begin to mend.
A flicker of hope in a heartbeat so faint,
Ensnared by the beauty of night's soft complaint.

With every soft sigh, the stars start to fade,
Painting the sky in a delicate shade.
Ghosts of the day whisper secrets unheard,
Their tales linger long, though their presence deferred.

The chill in the air wraps the earth like a cloak,
Whispers of spirits, in soft echoes spoke.
Their laughter, a promise, though fleeting it seems,
Guiding the dreamers through nightmarish dreams.

Yet from every shadow, a glimmer persists,
A truth hidden deep in the heart of the mist.
The dying light's warmth speaks of love so divine,
Reminding the wary of the strength in the line.

So linger a moment, embrace the soft glow,
For where hope is tethered, the heart starts to grow.
In the dance of the dying, life starts to renew,
A spark in the darkness, waiting for you.

Twilight's Silhouette on the Enchanted Pond

In twilight's embrace, where the waters gleam,
A silhouette dances, weaving a dream.
A whisper of magic, the lapping of tides,
On the enchanted pond, where mystery abides.

Fragrant blooms gather in the dusk's gentle sigh,
Reflecting a canvas painted by the sky.
Ripples of laughter float soft through the air,
Where moments are captured, serene and rare.

The stars hold their breath, witnessing the play,
Of shadows and light in a dance, a ballet.
Each whisper of wind carries tales from afar,
Illuminating paths where the fireflies are.

In the hush of the evening, a sweet serenade,
A symphony crafted in starlit cascade.
Twilight enchants every heart that draws near,
To the enchanted pond where the dreams persevere.

So linger, dear wanderer, 'neath the soft light,
Embrace the enchantment that cradles the night.
For in every shadow, a promise unfolds,
In twilight's silhouette, a story is told.

The Last Flicker of Enchantment

In the twilight, shadows play,
Whispers of magic glide away.
Hopes that danced on silken threads,
Fade like dreams in quiet beds.

Once bright flames now flicker low,
Lost to time, they gently go.
Echoes of joy, so soft and sweet,
In the hush, the heart's soft beat.

Promises made under the stars,
Burdens now feel like rusty bars.
Yet still, the heart keeps yearning fast,
For a glimpse of enchantment past.

Tales of wonder on winds do ride,
Secret paths where hopes abide.
In twilight's glow, we hold our breath,
Awaiting whispers from beyond death.

But as the night wears on and sighs,
We gather dreams beneath the skies.
With every flicker, hope survives,
In shadows deep, enchantment thrives.

Faint Glimmers on the Faerie Furl

Beneath the leaves, a soft light glows,
Where gentle streams of silver flows.
In hidden glades, where wildflowers bloom,
Faerie laughter dispels all gloom.

Faint glimmers trace the winding paths,
Leading hearts away from wrath.
With each step on the emerald green,
Secrets whisper, barely seen.

In shadows deep, where dreams take flight,
Spirits dance in the soft twilight.
Cotton clouds and whispers near,
Echoes of laughter, sweet and clear.

Through petals soft, and starlit beams,
We weave again our silver dreams.
A world beyond, of magic pure,
In every sigh, a memory sure.

When dawn arrives, our hearts will soar,
Carrying tales of faerie lore.
For in each glimmer of twinkling light,
We find our way through endless night.

Nostalgia in the Moonlit Clearing

In a clearing kissed by moon's soft glow,
Memories flit like fireflies in slow.
Twinkling softly, they call my name,
Echoes of joy, never the same.

Silence wraps the world in a sigh,
As shadows dance and whispers pry.
The trees stand tall, with tales to share,
Breath of the past, sweet and rare.

In this moment, time stands still,
With dreams and wishes, hearts to fill.
Familiar faces, lost in mists,
In moonlit circles, fate still twists.

Cupped in hands, the starlight gleams,
Rekindling fragments of forgotten dreams.
Each heartbeat echoes of days gone by,
As silver tears blend with the sky.

Nostalgia weaves its gentle spell,
In moonlit dance, we find farewell.
Yet in the dark, hope gently thrills,
For magic lingers, and hope fulfills.

Dimming Stars in the Faerie Realm

As twilight falls, the stars grow dim,
In secret glades where fairies skim.
Whispers linger on the evening air,
Tales of wonder, shimmers rare.

In their glow, the night feels old,
Stories spun, like threads of gold.
Moments lost in time's embrace,
Fleeting smiles on every face.

The nightingale sings a mournful tune,
As shadows deepen beneath the moon.
Softly, gently, the magic fades,
Where once were dreams, now mere cascades.

Yet deep within, a flicker stays,
A fire's warmth that never decays.
For in their plight and whispered screams,
We hold on tight to fading dreams.

So let the stars grow dim and fade,
In heart's embrace, their light is laid.
For even as the darkness nears,
The faerie realm will soothe our fears.

Wandering Through Enchanted Shadows

In twilight's cradle, dreams take flight,
Beneath the trees, where whispers invite.
Footsteps soft on ancient ground,
Secrets lost in silence found.

Moonbeams glisten on silver leaves,
Where every heart the night deceives.
Through winding paths and shadows deep,
The forest breathes, the stars will weep.

A flicker here, a sighing breeze,
Echoes linger among the trees.
Wandering souls with hopes to bind,
Enchanted realms of the wandering mind.

With every turn, the magic swells,
In whispers soft, the darkness tells.
Of fairy tales and fabled lore,
Where enchantment calls you to explore.

And as the night begins to fade,
The shadows dance, the glimmers wade.
In swirling mists and ghostly glows,
The magic's pulse forever flows.

Flickers of Enigma at Dusk

When dusk wraps all in velvet veils,
And mystery weaves its winding trails,
Flickers of light, a fleeting chance,
A dance of dreams, an ancient romance.

Through arches woven with ivy's grace,
Brushes of twilight on every face.
The air grows thick with unspoken words,
As secrets flit like startled birds.

Beneath the boughs, a shadow glides,
Whispers linger where magic abides.
A glimmer of hope, a question posed,
In the heart of night, all is exposed.

Past twilight's door, beyond the known,
A symphony of stars is grown.
With every heartbeat, time stands still,
The essence of dusk, the bend of will.

In phantoms bright, our spirits soar,
Through realms unseen, we seek for more.
Flickers of mystery, captivating dusk,
In every breath, the night we trust.

The Dimmed Echoes of Through the Glade

In the stillness of the fading light,
Echoes lilt on the edge of night.
Through the glade, where shadows leer,
Whispers of tales forgotten here.

A rustle deep within the trees,
Inhaling tales on the gentle breeze.
The paths we tread, now dimmed with time,
Resound with echoes, a haunting rhyme.

With every step, the echoes breathe,
Revealing wonders that we bequeath.
Lost in the melody of dreams,
The moonlit glade, where the starlight beams.

A tapestry sewn with threads of night,
Shimmers softly in silver light.
In every shadow, a story sleeps,
In the heart of the forest, silence weeps.

The past enveloped in a gentle shroud,
Where whispers blend, unruly and loud.
The dimmed echoes, a haunting song,
Guide the weary to where dreams belong.

Murmurs of Magic Among the Withered Boughs

Amidst the crones of withered boughs,
Where time has carved its solemn brows,
Murmurs rise like a hidden stream,
With riddles laced in a fleeting dream.

Here magic thrums in the sunset glow,
As if the world has started to grow.
A dance of shadows, a flicker of light,
Hiding the wonders of the night.

Ancient spirits weave through the air,
A tapestry woven with gentle care.
In every rustle, in every sigh,
The heartbeats of magic dance nearby.

Beneath the gnarled and twisted roots,
Whispers of magic wear leafy boots.
Among the boughs, secrets are spun,
Beneath a sky where the stars have begun.

Lost in the tangles, the weary find,
Murmurs of magic, softly entwined.
Among the withered, hope takes flight,
In every shadow, the spark of light.

The Last Flicker of Glittering Reverie

In shadows soft, the dreams still dance,
With wishes woven, in twilight's trance.
A whispered laugh, a fleeting grace,
The last flicker of a starry place.

Like embers warm, the memories glow,
In secret corners, where whispers flow.
The heart remembers what time forgets,
In lingering scents of sweet regrets.

A glimmering path through silver mist,
Each step a choice, impossible to resist.
The night unveils what daylight obscures,
In this flicker, our soul endures.

With candlelight dreams that gently sway,
The legends of old lead us astray.
Through realms of wonder, we shall roam,
In this flicker's warmth, we find our home.

As dawn approaches, the night must yield,
The resplendent dreams, forever sealed.
Yet in our hearts, the glow will stay,
The last flicker guides our way.

Fractured Illusions of the Enchanted Woods

In tangled vines, the secrets lie,
Where echoes linger, and shadows sigh.
Beneath the boughs of ancient trees,
Fractured illusions drift on the breeze.

A tender murmur, a haunting call,
The whispers weave through the forest hall.
With every step, the magic swells,
In this realm where the wild things dwell.

Moonlight spills like silver wine,
And time itself begins to entwine.
In the heart of the woods, the world grows tall,
Fractured illusions that charm us all.

A playful sprite, with mischievous glee,
Teases the wanderers, setting hearts free.
Yet every laughter hides a tear,
In enchanted woods, love's closest fear.

When morning comes, the magic fades,
But in our souls, the essence stays.
Through fractured paths in the leaves, we find,
In the enchanted woods, our dreams aligned.

Nightfall's Song in the Veil of Whimsy

As daylight bows in soft retreat,
The world transforms, at twilight's feet.
In a veil of whimsy, shadows swirl,
Nightfall's song begins to unfurl.

With silver stars like diamonds bright,
Each twinkling tune ignites the night.
A serenade for the wandering heart,
In the magic of dusk, we find our part.

The moon takes stage, both bold and shy,
Bathing the world in her tender sigh.
Dreamers awaken to the gentle plea,
In the veil of whimsy, we are forever free.

The playful winds hum softly low,
Secrets of night we long to know.
With every note, enchantments rise,
In the song of night, our spirit flies.

As darkness deepens, we hold each sound,
In whispers lost, where dreams abound.
Nightfall's song, a cherished thread,
In the veil of whimsy, we are led.

Eerie Blossoms of the Gathering Twilight

In gardens where no sunlight streams,
The eerie blossoms weave their dreams.
With petals dark as whispered fears,
They bloom beneath the watchful years.

A fog descends, serene and still,
The air is thick with hidden will.
Each flower sways, a ghostly dance,
In the twilight's glow, we take our chance.

With fragrant sighs that chill the spine,
These blooms unravel the sacred line.
In every shadow, stories breathe,
In the gathering twilight, we believe.

An old enchantress hums her tune,
Among the petals, beneath the moon.
We linger long, with hearts entwined,
Eerie blossoms, fate inclined.

When darkness falls, we'll make our vows,
Among the sights where daylight bows.
In these eerie blooms, the night ignites,
The beauty of fragile, fleeting sights.

Fading Light Over the Eldritch Meadow

The twilight whispers secrets low,
As shadows stretch and softly grow.
Amidst the grass, the faeries play,
In dimming hues of end-the-day.

A dance of shadows, laughter clear,
The moon ascends, the sun disappears.
Underneath the ancient boughs,
Time stands still, the world allows.

In every breeze, a tale untold,
Of realms where mysteries unfold.
The stars ignite, a silver thread,
Weaving dreams where none have tread.

The meadow hums a haunting tune,
As night envelops all too soon.
With every step, a promise fades,
In the embrace of twilight shades.

Yet in the hush, a spark remains,
A flicker bright amidst the chains.
In fading light, we find our way,
To chase the dusk, to greet the day.

Glistening Fragments of a Lost Realm

In chasms deep where echoes lie,
A glimmer breaks the endless sigh.
Fragments twinkle, lost and free,
Whispers of what used to be.

Through veils of mist, a path appears,
Guiding us through dreams and fears.
A world adorned in shades of gray,
Where light once danced, now fades away.

Each shard reflects a story past,
Each memory, a spell cast.
In corners curled, the magic sleeps,
In twilight's hold, the silence weeps.

A tapestry of lost delight,
Threads of hope in darkest night.
A flicker calls from long ago,
To brave the depths, to rise and glow.

Yet still we search, through endless time,
For glistening pieces, hopes that rhyme.
In shadowed realms, the quest begins,
To find the light where love once wins.

Yearning in the Glade of Forgotten Leaves

In the glade where shadows dance,
Whispers curl in nature's trance.
Leaves of ember, brown and gold,
Frame the tales the ancients told.

Beneath the boughs, the silence sighs,
Echoing hearts and lonely cries.
In every rustle, a memory stirs,
Of distant dreams and gentle spurs.

The moonlight spills on paths unseen,
Illuminating what has been.
Yearning breathes beneath the trees,
A longing carried on the breeze.

Each step recalls a fleeting glance,
Of tangled roots and fateful chance.
In the glade, the past entwines,
A fragrant air where history shines.

Yet still we linger, still we roam,
For in this place, we find our home.
In whispers soft, the glade will weave,
A tapestry of love we grieve.

The Lament of Withering Petals

Once vibrant blooms with colors bright,
Now drift away in fading light.
Each petal falls a silent sigh,
As time's embrace draws ever nigh.

In gardens lush where life once thrived,
Hope lingers on, though dreams have died.
The fragrance lost, the beauty wanes,
As seasons shift and memory remains.

Each drooping stem a silent plea,
For moments lost, for what could be.
In tender whispers, shadows fade,
A soft lament, a heart betrayed.

Yet still the earth holds deep its grief,
In roots and soil, the hope for relief.
A cycle turns, a new dawn brews,
From withering petals, life renews.

And though the blooms may fade away,
Their essence haunts the light of day.
In every bloom, a truth we find,
A dance of love, the ties that bind.